Fact Finders®

Teachers, that means Laugh Out Loud.
Yup, science can be hilarious!

LOL Physical Science

The GRIPPING TRUTH about FORCES and MOTION

by Agnieszka Biskup
illustrated by Bernice Lum

A motion joke:
A snail was crossing the road.
Suddenly it was run over by
a turtle. When the snail
woke up, a doctor asked what
happened. The snail replied,
"I don't know. It all happened
so fast."

None of these super cool people
were forced to work on this book.
They know science is cool.
And soon ... so will you!

Consultant:
Alec Bodzin
Associate Professor of Science Education
Lehigh University
Bethlehem, Pennsylvania

CAPSTONE PRESS
a capstone imprint

Fact Finders are published by Capstone Press,
1710 Roe Crest Drive, North Mankato, Minnesota 56003.
www.capstonepub.com

Library of Congress Cataloging-in-Publication Data
Biskup, Agnieszka.
The gripping truth about forces and motion / by Agnieszka Biskup; illustrated by
Bernice Lum.
p. cm.—(Fact finders. LOL physical science)
Summary: "Describes what forces are and how motion works through humor and core
science content"—Provided by publisher.
Includes bibliographical references and index.
ISBN 978-1-4296-8601-3 (lib. bdg.)—ISBN 978-1-4296-9298-4 (pbk.)
ISBN 978-1-62065-240-4 (ebook pdf)
1. Force and energy—Juvenile literature. 2. Motion—Juvenile literature. I. Lum,
Bernice, ill. II. Title.
QC73.4.B489 2013
531'.11—dc23   2011052723

Editorial Credits
Jennifer Besel, editor; Tracy Davies McCabe, designer; Svetlana Zhurkin, media
    researcher; Laura Manthe, production specialist

Photo Credits
Dreamstime: Didier Kobi (blackboard), 14; iStockphoto: Andriy Petrenko, 20 (front),
Stacey Walker, cover and throughout (frame), 4 (window); Shutterstock: Alexey
Stiop, 4 (back), 28 (back), Augusto Cabral (cartoon eyes), 15, Csdesign, 29, Danny
Smythe (apple), 15, DM7 (robot), back cover, 24, dutourdumonde, 20 (back), Freeky
(building), 10, Genestro, 12, giorgiomtb, 8, Iriana Shiyan, 21 (back), JinYoung Lee,
18, Jut, 11 (back), Kim Reinick, 17, mart (pencil scribbles), cover and throughout,
Mastertasso, 22 (front), Mikhail (car), back cover, 24, Nicku, 15 (bottom), Olga
Tropinina (arrows and speech bubbles), cover and throughout, Olivier Le Queinec,
27 (right), sdecoret, 22 (back), Skyline (notebook sheet), cover and throughout, ssguy
(background), cover and throughout, Studio Barcelona (sun), 10, Tomislav Forgo
(shopping cart), 7, tuulijumala (explosion), 3 and throughout, Vladyslav Danilin,
27 (left)

Printed in the United States of America.
082019   002412

TABLE (OF) CONTENTS

Move It!

Have you ever pretended to be a statue? Try standing perfectly still. Don't move a muscle. Can you do it? It's not that easy. Your chest is rising and falling as you breathe. Your heart is beating. And it's definitely getting harder not to blink! Your body is constantly in motion, even when you try your best not to move.

Now go ahead and unfreeze yourself. Walk to the window. You'll see even more things in motion. Tree leaves wave. Clouds float by. Birds fly. Dogs chase Frisbees. Cars whiz past. And these are just the things you can see from your window.

The universe is filled with motion, from the biggest to the smallest things. Giant planets spin around the Sun, and galaxies rotate in space. Teeny, tiny fleas jump from pet to pet. Microscopic germs try to wriggle up your nose.

Does anyone really try things that books tell them to do? I mean, it's not like the book knows if you do it or not.

This is assuming your window doesn't just give you a view of your neighbors' building. If that's the case, you'll obviously need to try another window.

Do you need a tissue now? :)

All the objects in the universe move or can be made to move. But what causes all that movement?

Chapter 1

Forcing the Issue

Nothing can move without something called a force acting on it. Really, nothing at all! But what is a force?

A force is simply a push or pull on an object. When a frog leaps off a lily pad, its legs **exert** a force on the plant. When you push a shopping cart, you're using a force to move it forward. If you give the cart a gentle push, it will move a little. Give it a great big shove, and you can see how much farther it will go. The greater the force, the greater the motion!

Machines can produce larger forces than we can with our muscles. Rocket engines produce forces millions of times stronger than the force you use pushing a shopping cart.

Forces in real life have nothing to do with Jedi.

exert—to make an effort to do something

Forces can also stretch a rubber band, tear a piece of paper, bend a spoon, or squash a pillow. They can stop a moving car or speed it up. Forces can make a ball bounce and make a top spin.

Forces are acting all around you, all the time. You can't see them, but they're there.

They're not putting on a play. It's not that kind of acting.

Stop Pushing! (If You Can)

Objects apply forces on each other →
all the time. Even when you're standing still,
the ground is exerting a force up to you,
supporting your body. This supporting force is
called the normal force. In this case normal means
perpendicular, not the opposite of strange.

But don't look so innocent. You're exerting a
force down on the ground too. How big your force
is depends on how much you weigh. Say your
body pushes down on the ground with 50 pounds
(23 kilograms) of force. The ground pushes back
with that same amount of normal force.

But wait, there's more!
Other forces are acting on you
too. The air is squeezing your
body from every direction.
But the matter in your body is
pushing right back at the air.

Parents apply forces
all the time too.
Forcing you to clean
your room, do the
dishes, finish your
homework ...

perpendicular—straight up and down relative to another surface; the two
lines that form the letter T are perpendicular to each other

And **gravity**, that most famous force of all, is acting on you too. Try to jump up in the air. It's gravity's force that pulls you down. Without gravity you'd be floating around the ceiling of your room right now.

Floating while reading this book would be way more fun. Thanks for nothing, gravity.

gravity—a force that pulls objects with mass together

The Gravity of the Situation

Gravity is the force of **attraction** between objects. All objects have a gravitational force. Even you have the force! But the bigger the object, the stronger its gravitational pull. A giant skyscraper has some gravitational pull. But the pull is not so big that we notice it when we walk by. An object has to be pretty darn big for us to be able to feel it. Earth, for example, is pretty big. Its gravitational pull is strong. Earth's gravity keeps us from floating off its surface. It also holds the Moon in orbit and our **atmosphere** in place.

Now think about the Sun. The Sun's gravity is what keeps our solar system together. It attracts Earth and all the other planets.

Random Space Fact: If the Sun was hollow, more than 1 million Earths could fit inside.

attraction—the act of being pulled toward something
atmosphere—the mixture of gases that surrounds Earth

The strength of an object's gravity is determined by its mass. To really understand forces and motion, you have to understand what mass really is.

That's your cue to turn the page.

Mass Matters

Mass is the amount of stuff that makes up an object. All objects have mass. Some things have a lot of mass, while others have less. For example, a moose has a lot more mass than a bird. Earth has more mass than the Moon.

That "stuff" in mass is called matter. Matter is what makes up every single thing in the universe. The air we breathe is made of matter. Every star, planet, and galaxy is made of matter. And everything alive is made of matter too. Matter is anything that has mass and takes up space.

I matter!

I have mass and take up space. So I matter too!

So the moral of the story is that no matter your size, YOU matter too.

Mass vs. Weight

People often think of mass and weight as the same thing. But they're not! Mass stays the same wherever you are in the universe. But an object's weight can change. Weight is actually a measurement of the gravitational pull on an object. If you weigh 100 pounds on Earth, Earth's gravity is pulling you down with 100 pounds of force. But the Moon has a weaker gravitational pull. So if you were there, you'd only weigh about 17 pounds. On our massive Sun, you'd weigh a whopping 2,800 pounds!

That is, if you could stand on it without being burned up.

If you weigh 100 pounds (45 kg) on Earth, what would you weigh in space?

Place	What Would You Weigh?
Pluto	7 pounds (3 kg)
Moon	17 pounds (8 kg)
Mars	38 pounds (17 kg)
Mercury	38 pounds (17 kg)
Uranus	80 pounds (36 kg)
Venus	90 pounds (41 kg)
Saturn	93 pounds (42 kg)
Neptune	120 pounds (54 kg)
Jupiter	254 pounds (115 kg)
Sun	2,800 pounds (1,270 kg)

Chapter 2

Obey the Laws

Gravity has always existed, but it took people time to figure out what it was and how it worked. In 1687 English scientist Isaac Newton published a book about his amazing discoveries. In it he explained his law of universal gravitation. He recognized that gravity was a force that existed everywhere in the universe. Newton realized that gravity caused the motion of the planets, and it was responsible for falling objects on Earth. He showed how the force of gravitational attraction between two objects depended on two things.

1. Distance: The greater the distance, the smaller the force pulling objects together.

2. Mass:
The greater the mass of the objects, the greater the force of gravity.

Newton also discovered three simple laws that describe how forces make things move. Newton's laws can be used to explain the movement of all objects in the universe. Those three laws are discussed on the following pages.

Fig Newtons are not named after the scientist Isaac Newton. The cookies are named for a town in Massachusetts, which was not named after the scientist either.

But those three laws don't explain the laws of motion in cartoons.

Legend has it that an apple fell on Newton's head. Then he magically thought of his gravity laws.

However, the same method has never helped students with schoolwork.

Number 1

Newton's first law is the law of **inertia**. Inertia means that an object tends to stay at rest if it's at rest. Or an object in motion will stay in motion. Of course, this is true unless the object is acted on by some outside force.

The more mass something has, the more inertia it has. It's a lot harder to move a massive sleeping elephant than a tiny sleeping bug.

It makes sense that something stays still until you push or pull it. But what about something staying in motion if it's already in motion? On Earth things don't keep moving forever. They slow down. But what causes that slow down? It's caused by a force called **friction**.

Newton's First Law according to a fourth grader: A body in motion stays in motion. A body at rest stays in bed unless its mom forces it to get up.

Friction occurs when two objects come in contact with one another. Every object has microscopic bumps and lumps. When two things rub together, these rough pieces catch on each other. This catching causes objects to slow down. The rougher something is, the more friction it creates. So if you shot a hockey puck on rough grass, it would slow down pretty quickly. But shoot it on smooth ice, and the puck slides for a longer time.

Grass hockey would be a pretty slow game. Maybe parents would like it.

inertia—an object's state in which the object stays at rest or keeps moving in the same direction until a greater force acts on the object

friction—a force created when two objects rub together; friction slows down objects

Number 2

Get your mind out of the toilet. This isn't about poop.

Up next is Newton's second law of motion. This law says that when a force acts on an object, the object's movement will change. It will start to move, speed up, slow down, or change direction. The more force you apply, the greater the change in movement. But mass also has a part to play. The more mass an object has, the more force it takes to move it.

Newton came up with a formula to help explain his law.

force = mass x acceleration

People usually think of **acceleration** as an increase in speed. But acceleration is really any change in speed. So speeding up, slowing down, and even changing direction are all accelerations.

Roller coasters accelerate the speed of my vomit.

This is one of those facts that even many adults don't know. That's right. You are now smarter than most adults. You're welcome.

acceleration—the change in speed or direction of a moving body

18

Newton's second law says that you need a big force to accelerate a massive object. A toy truck with little mass is easier to accelerate than a real truck.

The law also says that the greater the force on an object, the faster it will accelerate. Kick a toy truck gently, and it will roll slowly. Kick it harder, and the toy truck will roll faster.

We don't recommend trying this experiment on a real truck.

Number 3

Newton's third law is probably his most famous. This law says for every action there is an equal but opposite reaction. By actions, Newton means forces.

Forces never occur alone. They always come in pairs. If one object pushes another, the second object pushes back with the same amount of force. It's just like the normal force you read about earlier.

You DID read that, right?

Think of it like this. If you push against a wall, the wall is pushing back at you with the same amount of force. You could check this out by wearing roller skates and pushing against the same wall. You'd travel backward because the wall pushed back at you.

The best things in life come in pairs:
socks
Popsicles
chopsticks
pants

Want another good example of Newton's third law? Blow up a balloon, and then let it go. The force of air coming out of the balloon is equal to the force of the balloon zooming around the room.

You do know that beans aren't really a magical fruit, right?

That sound isn't what you think ...

phhhhht!

What did the balloon say to the pin?

Hi, Buster!

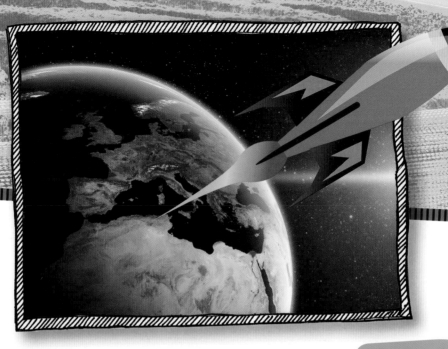

The Law's on Your Side

Yes, even you. You just DIDN'T KNOW WHAT you WERE DOING until now. Again, you're welcome.

People use Newton's laws every day. Think about the rockets that send astronauts into space. Rockets use Newton's third law. A rocket pushes gas out of its engines. Then the gas pushes back on the rocket and lifts it into space.

Scientists also use what Newton learned about distance's affect on gravity. The greater the distance, the smaller the force pulling objects together. So if a force can get the rocket far enough away, Earth's gravity can't pull it back.

Scientists call the pull of gravity during acceleration g-force. A **stationary** object has a g-force of 1. Sitting still, reading this book, you're feeling 1 g. But just like in Newton's second law, you can experience more g-force by accelerating.

Have you ever been in a car that took off quickly? That quick acceleration caused a g-force that pushed you back into your seat. Roller coasters can put up to 5 g's on your body. Even sitting down really fast puts 10.1 g's on your body for just a short time.

Obviously g stands for gravity, not gerbils.

Activity	G's felt momentarily
sneezing	2.9
slap on the back	4.1
jump from 3 feet (.9 meter) and land with stiff legs	100

Achooo!

stationary—not moving

23

Chapter 3

Force It

You use forces all the time in everyday life, pushing and pulling objects. But sometimes you need a force that's bigger than what your muscles can provide. That's when you can use a machine.

Machines to the rescue!

Machines reduce the amount of force needed to do work. We're not talking about homework here. In this case, work means to apply a force to an object and move it a distance. Scientifically speaking, work is defined as force times distance.

Everybody else defines work as stuff that's not fun to do. Scientists always have to make things complicated.

We really have no idea what this picture is about. It's just really cool, so we added it here. It's like a machine lifting a machine.

But there's a catch when it comes to machines doing work. If the machine applies a large force, the force can only be applied over a short distance. But if it uses a smaller force, it needs to apply that force over a greater distance to complete the work. Turn the page to see how this trade-off works with simple machines.

Really. Turn tHe page.
NotHing else is going to Happen Here.
Ok, use your Hand to apply force to
tHis page, anD turn tHe page over.

Not-So-Simple Machines

Some machines are so simple you might not even consider them machines. Ramps, wedges, and screws are machines that are used to do work. These machines can make jobs easier to do because they allow a change in the force. But in all these machines, you have the force-distance trade-off.

Ramps, also known as inclined planes, are the simplest kinds of machines. Ancient Egyptians used ramps to help build the pyramids. It's a lot easier to push a 2-ton (1.8-metric ton) stone up a ramp than to lift it straight up. But the trade-off is that you have to push the stone a farther distance than if you did just lift it.

I think the Egyptians would agree that pushing giant stones up ramps is no picnic either.

Yes, we agree that this is no picnic.

Enough with the simple machines. When do we get some complicated ones?

Wedges are powerful. The blade of an ax is a wedge. Swing an ax into wood. The force of that long downward swing is turned into powerful, but short, sideways forces. Those forces split the wood.

Wedgies are powerful forces too but not for the same reasons.

Screws are simply inclined planes wrapped around cylinders. With each turn, a screwdriver pushes a screw a bit farther into a piece of wood. But the screw applies a much greater force than your hand alone could apply. There's a trade-off, though. The screw only goes in a fraction of an inch for each full turn of the screwdriver.

Using a screwdriver instead of your hand is far less painful too.

It's Complicated

Eventually, inventors started putting simple machines together to create complicated ones. Complex machines include motorcycles, cars, elevators, and more. Instead of muscle power, complex machines are driven by engines or motors. But Newton's three laws still apply to the forces and motion of these machines too.

Forces and motion surround you every day. From the force used to fill your lungs to the force keeping Earth in orbit, we can't escape forces and motion.

But without the pushes and pulls of forces, life as we know it wouldn't be possible. Without gravity, for example, Earth wouldn't have an atmosphere. There'd be no air to breathe.

Yeah, but wouldn't it be fun to float on the ceiling?

Three cheers for forces and motion!

Hurray! Hurray! Hurray!

Well, that's about the dumbest book conclusion ever. Sorry.

Glossary

acceleration (ak-sel-uh-RAY-shuhn)—the change in speed or direction of a moving body

atmosphere (AT-muhss-fihr)—the mixture of gases that surrounds Earth

attraction (uh-TRAK-shun)—the act of being pulled toward something

cylinder (SIL-uhn-dur)—a shape with flat, circular ends and sides shaped like a tube

exert (eg-ZURT)—to make an effort to do something

friction (FRIK-shuhn)—a force created when two objects rub together; friction slows down objects

gravity (GRAV-uh-tee)—a force that pulls objects with mass together

inertia (in-UR-shuh)—an object's state in which the object stays at rest or keeps moving in the same direction until a greater force acts on the object

perpendicular (pur-puhn-DIK-yuh-lur)—straight up and down relative to another surface; the two lines that form the letter T are perpendicular to each other

stationary (STAY-shuh-ner-ee)—not moving

Read More

Dicker, Katie. *Forces and Motion.* Sherlock Bones Looks at Physical Science. New York: Windmill Books, 2011.

Evans Ogden, Lesley J. *Forces and Motion.* Physical Science. New York: AV2 by Weigl, 2012.

Weakland, Mark. *Zombies and Forces and Motion.* Monster Science. Mankato, Minn.: Capstone Press, 2012.

Internet Sites

FactHound offers a safe, fun way to find Internet sites related to this book. All of the sites on FactHound have been researched by our staff.

Here's all you do:

Visit *www.facthound.com*

Type in this code: 9781429686013

Super-cool stuff!

Check out projects, games and lots more at
www.capstonekids.com

Index